DRAWING BACK

Poems Written in the Autumn of 2025

By
Lester Hirsh

Parisburg Publishing

ISBN: 978-1-61918-074-1

First Edition

Front Cover Art: *Remembering Fall*, by Lessie Carbonneau
Inside Art: *From a Canoe* and *Bamboo*, by Lessie
Carbonneau (Hudson, Fla.) *Man Leaning on Shadow—*
Lester Hirsh

Inside Quote: F. Scott Fitzgerald
Pulling Poems for Inspiration line-with eggs golden as
drops of grain, attributed to Sharon Olds

Web sites and email:
 www.parisburg.beone.ws/lesterhirsh.htm,
www.bignoisenow.com/hirsh.html and
lesterhirsh@hotmail.com

Essential Graphic formatting by Walter Dolen.
Thanks also to Michael DeMarco of Bloomsburg, Pa
for invaluable time transferring the book in Thumb Drive
format. Hirsh is also associated with his Zen Napkin Press.

Parisburg Publishing
Pennsylvania

OTHER OFFERINGS BY LESTER HIRSH

Books: Photographs & Letters (1982)

Mosaic II: Poems of An Ancient Order (1999)

Sketchbook - (2010)

Lyrics of a Troubadour- (2013)

Mexican Mosaics - (2014)

The Imagined Gift- (2025)

Albums:

Three LP Tapes: Part & Parcel (1986) Piper's Dream (1990) Whistle in the Wind (1994)

CD'S: Tales of a Troubadour (1994)- Sweet Surrender (1998)

Strangers or Lonesome Friends (2003) Lester Hirsh Live at the Coffee & Tea Room (2005)

Spoken Word CD- Mosaic ii: Poems of An Ancient Order (2005) Volumes I and II

Instrumental CD'S- River of Strings (2006) Arpeggio (2017)

The Other Side Of Folk- An Album of Traditional & Classic Folk Songs of Other Songwriters (2015)

Fractured Suite- Live Acoustic Tracks written & composed by Lester Hirsh (2019)

Dedication

To the Memories of

Rick Abrams

Fleur Byers

Louis Tertocha

From a Canoe — Lessie Carbonneau

Table of Contents

So we beat on,
boats against the current,
born back ceaselessly into the past.

F. Scott Fitzgerald
(The Great Gatsby)

Bamboo — Lessie Carbonneau

Trolling

Which nightmare should we dive into? The one in which you are running around some foreign town in the tropics like a vagabond with no sense of where you really are or where you are going.

How about the one where you are talking with your deceased mother as if she was a passenger in the car you are driving through a stretch of endless night, and it seems so real that when you awake you feel certain the dream was more real than the illusion of reality outside the dream.

Or what about the dilemma of running away from yesteryears ghost. That witch from the Wizard of Oz, flying on her broomstick in a cloud that later shows up on your bedroom wall, excoriating you for not following her diabolic demands that you not abandon her, that night you were sleepwalking staring at the bedroom wall as a kid in that dark coal town, when you fell back to bed, hitting your head on the pillow seeing stars like fireworks in front of your face, after which you raced into your parents' room to sleep between them, then slept with a nightlight on for another five years or more.

Even now those dreams troll you like the bogeyman behind the bedroom door and you often awake at 3 in the morning, that hour the writer F. Scott Fitzgerald wrote about as being the real dark night of the soul, and you turn on that switch in the hallway or the closet to sleep in the half- light for the sake of your sanity until morning comes as a sigh of relief.

Memories in the Mirror

I used to take my mother to her Temple
for the last hour of the Sabbath Service,
mostly because it took her a long time
to eat, wash, and dress in the morning
when she was arthritic and slow moving
in her 90's.

Afterwards we would lunch at a Deli
on Hallandale Beach Boulevard,
often with her best friend Bess Selevin.

The Deli had breakfast and lunch specials
 fine bagel and lox smears that satiated the appetite.

Afterwards, we'd drive back to mother's condo
to while away afternoon hours,
where I'd nap in the den, then lounge
 on the outdoor 5th floor patio,
staring at high-rise buildings blocking
a clear view of the Atlantic Ocean
a few miles east of her Aventura home.

Later in the afternoon, we'd drive to my brother's house
off of 47th street on Miami Beach, and go with
his wife and their two kids,
to a restaurant or Deli
for dinner.

Back at their house, we'd watch a movie
lying on the couch with the terrier-poodle
after which I'd drive mother home on the old
familiar route past the hotel strip,
up through Surfside, and Sunny Isles,
then back to Aventura.

Along the route my mother and I would sit
in silence, or chat amicably about the future
which was certain to include the end of days
like a shadow around the corner that was only
a matter of time before it came unannounced.

Then Came November

In coal country I remember the bleakness,
skinny white birch trees that stood naked
on top of black hills by culm banks.

The tarred roofs of row houses
always looked damp and dreary.
Sidewalk cracks seemed more broken.

Fallen leaves that abandoned branches
in October, lay strewn on streets,
and blown about in the stiff wind.

We would walk uptown in our corduroy
pants, long sleeve shirts and jackets,
by clothing and shoe stores,
to check out Fall fashion window displays.

Before heading home we'd pass the
Capitol and Strand Theatre to check
the movie marquee for upcoming shows.

Town folk would make plans for
Thanksgiving and Christmas well in advance
of the light display downtown that would
stay up through the first weekend of the New Year.

I remember those days with mixed emotions,
when families huddled at home around the dinner table,
or later by the Philco TV screen watching sitcoms and holiday movies,
like White Christmas starring Bing Crosby.

Still, I withdrew more often than not,
thinking about fallen leaves blowing
in that stiff wind, white birch trees
on hilltops, the fall rain, leading up
to the longest night of the year.

Spending Time

I don't mind spending time alone
to clear cobwebs in the inner sanctum

To listen to that still small voice within
To meditate on a passing moment

Because moments cannot
be taken for granted

in this gift of life
for however long they last

To My Parents

I sometimes sense both of you, staring from that ether world,

in contemplation of my birth, that fashioned from your union.

Old as I am, you remember the infancy of that day,

through childhood, adolescence, into adulthood.

It is as though my life has passed through the channel

of a canal, on a journey guided by a gondolier,

with both of you there, smiling.

At times, when I am riding alone in the car,

I feel your presence,

like a gesture of reassurance that we,

are on this journey together.

I can hear the tone of your voices,

melodic, familiar, searching for definition,

from one world to the other,

a place and time when one day

we will meet again.

Drawing Back

Last night I drew back
into a dream of the past,

walking the streets
of that coal town
by the home we lived in.

The dream, an old film
In black and white,
reoccurs,

like an apparition
on Halloween,

but my ghosts visit,
more than once a year.

Short Poems

short poems
            are stepping stones
                        to what lies beneath them

unsung arias
no wife
or next of kin
a thousand if's
in the book of regrets

yet to dwell on loss
is poison to the heart

so best to keep
short poems short
when enough is said

Coloring

The morning sky has gray, blue, and pink shading,
set above rust- colored leaves left on fall trees.

In a world set on fire with warring factions and political
dissension, it brings a modicum of comfort, to know nature
ignores the folly of men,

waiting patiently for the day human madness parts
this piece of paradise, that fared well enough before our
arrival.

November Haunts

The pumpkins are no longer in the patch
and Halloween has already passed
but the ghosts of present- day dreams
continue to haunt the night

Sometimes it is a flight of fancy
as if out of an Indiana Jones movie
where Harrison Ford is on a quest
to find an ancient artifact
and you are with him
another guide on the precarious ride

At other times you are by the bedside
of your ailing old mother still holding
her hand through the ordeal of her passing

November, the month that lies
between the bedsheets of Fall and Winter
I think of the movie-Three Days of the Condor
the character Joe Turner, a CIA codebreaker
played by Robert Redford, who seeks refuge
in the New York City basement apartment
of photographer Kathy Hale, played by
Faye Dunaway, who Turner determines
is as elusive and non-committal
as November is transitional

November is a festive time as well,
a time to celebrate the Day of the Dead
as it is done each November in Mexico,
on the first and second days, to honor
deceased children, known as Dia de los
Angelitos

Then there are abundant harvest festivals,
a time to revel in the passing of fall
in anticipation of a New Year when winter winds
remind us the haunts of November past
still linger late into the night

November Is a Reminder

November is a reminder that death
lurks in the shadows,
when you learn your accountants' son
died in his sleep at the age of 55,
and another friend's atrial fibrillation
requires an immediate pacemaker
to keep her alive.

November has a look like a sinister
lady with rouge waiting to lure you
into a web of deception behind
her cold and calculating breath.

You think ahead to December
when your mother died on the 8th
of that month, how many years ago,
though you are still in the throes of November.

Something about November,
that mantra,
Say it again- November,
is a reminder, the tight rope
of life is a delicate balancing act,
so go dance the tango,
the samba, live life
as if today is the last moment
to celebrate the continuum
slipping through the hourglass,
despite the uncertainty of what
lies ahead, or the premonition
lodged in the heart of November,
as it passes with the prevailing wind.

Avalanche

 I've watched glaciers melt and avalanches
on a movie screen

the drift reminds me of civilization
always in flux

people being buried under banks
of caving earth in distress

and conflict, so much conflict,
warring tribes killing each other

for territorial gain or conquest
like stone age predators

another avalanche in the branch
of human history

Fortunes

I use to save paper wrappings
from Chinese fortune cookies
thinking maybe it was a fateful sign,
like people who read daily horoscopes
before stepping into the unfolding day.

Then I regarded the practice to be
mere superstition, a detrimental devise
as damning as a soothsayer's reading
of tarot cards.

The other day I found an old fortune
lying around my night desk by a stack
of books I read as a ritual before
turning off the evening light.

The fortune read: Everything you are
against weakens you. Everything you
are for empowers you.

I pondered the wisdom of that maxim
thinking it makes perfect sense, and
realized that was why I saved this fortune
for safekeeping.

Having said that, I'm still not going
to read the daily horoscopes,
rely on tarot cards,
or buy a bunch of fortune cookies
before stepping out the front door.

The Blue Heron

I first saw the bird standing in the shallow end of Muncy
Creek on the outskirts of Hughesville Pennsylvania,
in the summer of the late 1970's,
then a few decades later appearing resolute like a
feathered statue, by the banks of the Kanawha River in
Charleston, West Virginia.

Both times the bird looked solemn and contemplative.
I could only assume it was being its' solitary self,
or looking to find and breed with a mate,
as it stared across the water veering north,
seemingly oblivious to my distant presence.

I remember observing the heron like a birder who just
witnessed an unexpected sight unseen, in anticipation of
some quiet miracle about to unfold, but nothing so bold
and wondrous ever took place, no meeting of the birds'
mate, or anything else, in the time I spent staring out of
curiosity.

For that brief encounter, I longed to mindread the blue
heron, as if I could learn a lesson about the art of survival
in the wilds, from their intuitive intelligence, always alert
to any signs of danger, but the only revelation I stumbled
upon was that as a city dwelling human, I was simply out
of my element, and it was time for me to return to the
concrete jungle, and leave the heron well enough, alone.

Brushstroke

A tint of light enters the new morning
gray skies determine the days design
dreary and wet in November's forecast
somewhat similar in color
to a Vermeer painting

The bird in the rafters
above my bedroom ceiling
makes an audible sound
as if she too is waking from
a night of slumber

I write these words before
preparing morning coffee
and toasting a slice of flat bread
in the still quiet of early dawn

Hoping this day will be more
uneventful than not
as I plot the next line
to find its way in the margins
of this page

Safety Net

Nothing
In this one life
We have to live fully
Comes with a written guarantee
Nothing

The Book of Remembrances

Names and more names continue to crowd the pages

like miles and miles of headstones from the ruins

of civilization.

The wars have taken many to their graves,

the rest die from the consumption of life itself,

like Jonah being swallowed by the whale,

but this whale that swims in the sea of eternity

will not cough up the sorry lot of men

that fall prey through natural causes nor through

acts of violence, or wars of attrition.

The multitudes continue to be born

into a world of scorn or privilege,

but in the end, they all lie down with the humble,

and unknown soldier, hoping to be remembered,

on headstones, and books collecting dust on shelves,

where congregants once prayed to be saved

or at least not forgotten.

We Bow Our Heads

We bow our heads for the loss of life

of innocent children to the scourge of gunfire.

That crazy talk of citizen rights to own a firearm

like gold at Fort Knox.

What applied in the time of the Revolutionary War,

a few centuries later, is now an eyesore.

Stringent laws like brittle bones left unchecked

will break. If only we could change them

before it's too late.

The posturing of politicians, is an admission of guilt,

not an act of contrition, just a code of permission,

to carry on in the finest tradition,

citing founding fathers framing

the Constitution and Bill of Rights.

It's not a matter of one's right to bear arms,

but to keep innocent children and adults from indiscriminate
harm,

from dangerous weapons, meant for use on a battlefield,

not in our homes, on playgrounds, or in public schools.

Pennies from Heaven

What first comes to mind for you?
the hit song sung by Bing Crosby in 1936,
perhaps a gift from heaven or luck of the draw,
the day you won the lottery against all odds.

Perhaps, it was the day you learned your illness
was in remission, and you gave yourself permission,
to laugh, cry, and dance the night away.

Whatever the reason, the metaphor persists,
like the worn thin cliché- a penny saved is a penny earned,
loosely attributed to Benjamin Franklin who wrote in his
1737 Poor Richard's Almanack" A two pence saved, is two
pence clear."

It all comes down to the U.S. mint, who printed this year, the last
vestige of the penny coin on Wednesday, November 12, 2025,
at the Philadelphia facility. The final pennies will remain
uncirculated, and auctioned off. Certainly, they will be a
collectors' item in the numismatic world.

After a run of 232 years, the penny will go the way
of the Ford Edsel, produced in 1958 to 1960,
although there will be plenty of pennies still in circulation
for years to come, unlike the Edsel, one or two of which
are sometimes seen in antique car shows or museums.

Word has it, there are 250 billion pennies in circulation.
 As for the Song, Pennies from Heaven,
you can hum it any time, especially around the winter
holidays, when the ghost of Bing Crosby sings
on the radio and silver screen, as a reminder of the Golden
Age of Hollywood's bygone era.

Fitting In

It never felt quite right
growing up in the city,
a numberless face among the masses,
hanging out by burning neon lights,
in the pubs where dancing parties
took place, and perfumed girls
with their glittering gowns,
drank, sang, and danced
with fraternity friends,
through the heat of the night.

It always felt out of place,
trying to carve an identity
with the few friends I had,
who idled by the beach
or walked crowded streets
of Coconut Grove or South Beach,
like dead beats looking for action.

Adolescence was a tough time,
trying to make sense of it all,
especially after dad's death,
when I was fifteen,
and pondered what was left
to do when high school was through.

Memories of mining towns
were left in a warp of time,
behind the scrimmage line
of changing times, and I was never
that adept at handling change.

To a degree, fitting in never found
a home, until later in life,
when I took that inward turn,
to learn what suited me best,
sketching memories with my pen,
being around like-minded friends
who felt the same way I did,
valuing aesthetics over wealth,
or illusions of grandeur.

As a Kid on Coal Street

There was always a bleakness in November
when fallen leaves were strewn about
in the stiff air on town streets and sidewalks.
When short days felt like an omen of a pending death,
with the certainty that December would soon arrive.

We bundled up in hooded winter jackets
that kept our heads warm, while
rosy cheeks took the blunt of biting air
that danced inside our pants like polyester
flags on a flagpole.

Lots of folks anticipated the Christmas holiday,
exchanging gifts, festive food, watching movies,
hunkering down when the Northeaster blew
with snow and howling winds.

Afterwards, as winter dragged through the
corridor of New Year, the air seemed subdued,
and sad, as one would feel when a loved one passed,
and their presence would be longed for
but the euphoria could not last.

Then the lengthening days would slowly emerge,
with a surge of light and Valentine's Day around
the bend, when winter's end was near enough
to signal the coming of spring.

These were some of the things I remember
as a kid on coal street, in a small mining town
in the 1950's, before the advent of cell phones,
computers, and the internet, changed everything.

She Feels the Need

She feels the need to lord over her sorry sibling
leveraging the weight of wealth over his poverty.
Not a poverty of aesthetics, or profundity of poetic gifts,
but his ineptness in the depths of her financial bliss.

She feels the need to hold the gilded coins she's earned
in such high esteem, and nothing he could ever do or say
would change the way she dreams.

She feels the need to be on her pedestal,
and dare not concede that diamonds, like precious gold,
hold no value when a life is through, and he'd rather
be remembered for having left behind a good poem
or two.

A Nostalgic Drift

On a cold October night
in Ashland New Hampshire
from the bedroom perch
of Paul Hubert and Kathi Sheer's home
I slipped into a nostalgic drift

remembering that ivory moon
lighting the blackberry night
like a lantern above a ridge
of the White Mountains

driving on
to Marsha's trailer
in North Conway
after my gig at the Wildcat Inn
in the ski town of Jackson

temperature in the teens
a blast of arctic air
bundled in my winter coat
and corduroy cap

stopping at a convenience store
two in the morning
to grab a sandwich and chips

taking it back to the trailer
in the heart of darkness
and stifling air
drifting there
more than thirty years ago
another lifetime on the road

Overlooking Lake Winnipesaukee

With its pristine beauty, the lake reminds me
of the Sea of Galilee, an inlet by Tiberias
in the Holy Land

From the vantage point of a hill
The Presidential Range stands statuesque
in the backdrop, leading to
the pinnacle of Mt. Washington
above the skyline

The water in the lake paints a portrait
serene as a scene inside a picture frame
shades of azure blue water
mix in to match the fall foliage

I feel like floating in a rowboat there
where my imagination lifts all expectation
dreaming past the sunset and evening stars
that draw me nigh under the twilight sky

Fly fishing with Angus

For Angus Bozeman

It's been more than a decade since Angus
took me fly fishing in the New England northern tier
near the Canadian border.

It was the one and only time I had the experience
with the expertise of Angus to show me the angles
and art of fly fishing.

We were at the Tall Timber Lodge in Pittsburg,
New Hampshire, in the late spring of that year.

I remember wading in the streambed,
wearing waterproof boots up to my knees
under dungarees and a long sleeve shirt,
and that Angler cap to top things off.

I watched Angus cast his rod with hook
and bait swimming downstream, and how
soon thereafter he caught a small trout.

I followed suit and to my surprise,
hooked a fish that Angus let go.
Later, shortly before dusk,
we went back to the cabin
for a chicken dinner and chat.

I knew I'd not become a fly fisherman
like Hemingway and his son Jack,
but I still could revel being out
in the stream, with the cool water
massaging my calves and feet,
in the natural world,

being thankful to Angus
for a day and night reprieve,
like two stowaways escaping
the entrapment of the city,
her traffic and technology,
to enjoy fly fishing.

The Foggy Morning Mist

Sometimes I prefer the fog to sunshine
especially on fall mornings
when naked trees stand unabashed
like an exhibitionist on the landscape.

I drive into Lewisburg, that pristine
college town where Bucknell University lies,
some 9 miles down the road.

Driving through the center of town
with the morning mist insistent
on staying around until noon.

I'm playing the public radio station,
WVIA, broadcasting from Wilkes-Barre
an hour upstate in the Pocono Range.

First Vivaldi echoes through the airwaves,
setting the sentimental mood,
followed by Haydn, as I head
to the Giant grocery store.

After picking up a can of salmon,
salad, and shepherds' pie,
I head home on Route 15,
over to Milton, then Watsontown,
where I have lodged for the last decade.

By then, the sun has made a surprise
appearance, changing my mood
the somber tone on loan
from the foggy mist and morning dew.

I turn off the radio, and think about
the work I have to do, or procrastinate doing,
all the while wanting to write another poem,
a minor masterpiece I can share with poets
at the next reading.

The Mourning Dove

She started clearing her throat

before eight in the mourn

I was up earlier still

doing revisions on a poem

I was safe for an hour alone

before her cooing began

cowering from the rafters above

so much for peace and quiet

when I hear the mourning dove

When the World Spins Out of Control

When the world spins out of control

like wild horses running on the open plain

let it run the course and be porous

When your neighbor is burning steam

with a contrary point of view

let him say his peace

then walk away

Let the world spin the way it will

retreat inside yourself

Substance to Shadow

It's not unusual to know of someone
who is an overachiever.

A Renaissance man or woman
holding a number of degrees.

Someone adept at various skills
from home repairs to breaking horses.

A doctor, lawyer, or college professor
who earned an engineering degree.

The former President Teddy Roosevelt,
a prolific writer who wrote nearly 40 books.

William Carlos Williams, the pediatrician,
who won a Pulitzer Prize for his poetry.

So many people, renowned or not,
who quietly passed away in time,

from Substance to Shadow,
as we all eventually do.

Dreaming of the Tropics

It is usually this time of year

when the fierceness of Fall appears

and frost followed by a first snow

blanket the earth

as darkening days slip into twilight

that I begin to dream of the Tropics

I think of being in the warmth

lying down on a beach towel

looking out at the ocean

listening to the ripple of waves

breathing in soothing salt air

wishing I were there

Just the thought of a winter escape

drape my thoughts with redemption

a lesson in patience and perseverance

hoping for a reprieve, a midwinter's break

before the scent of spring arrives

America, In Thanksgiving Mode

Meanwhile, the homeless still huddle in shelters
and go to food banks for a meal, those that are
lucky enough to have food and shelter.

In other homes, the Thanksgiving meal is prepared
as it was last year, and the year before that.
Theres' enough food and dessert to stuff one's face,
and cause the belly to swell an inch or two.

It is said that 46 million turkeys are slaughtered each year
for consumption in the United States, with enough leftovers
to feed starving people in a corner of a third world nation.

I sometimes wonder what the Pilgrims who landed
In Plymouth, Massachusetts, would have thought
of our indulgent practices, like cannibals at a campfire.
The Pilgrims who came on the Mayflower voyage,
ate Indian corn, beans, and pumpkins. They hunted for
venison, fowl, and ate shellfish and cod.

But on the ship their main staple was a hardtack cracker,
salt pork, dried meat like cow tongue, oatmeal, and they
drank beer to avoid contaminated water.

Certainly, it was a far cry from prepared turkey, stuffing,
sweet potatoes, cooked carrots and corn, salad, bread,
cranberries, and enough dessert to satiate a sweet tooth,
and make a mockery of an earnest diet.

But Thanksgiving has become an American tradition, like
Apple pie, which I didn't mention before, or the All Vegetarian
meals some folks have who don't eat turkey or other meat.
So, let's indulge and be thankful again for what we still
have, because like the thin thread of freedom, we are
uncertain if our liberties, or fine cuisine, will be a given,
this time next year.

Every Now and Then

Every now and then
I get the urge to read a Charles Bukowski poem
like he had the urge to drink whiskey because
he was addicted to alcohol, or smoke his cigarettes,
because he had a nicotine addiction—

I know that sounds bitter,
that any addiction is hard to break
and in the long run is going to kill you—

but returning here to Charles Bukowski,
having just reread his poem
the knife waltz

in which he chain-smokes
pours whiskey into his shredded gut,
to use his words

and tells you people are not good
to one another,
while at the same time
he confesses to deserving

the evening
that leaves him depressed,
out of music, hope,
and cigarettes

but I remember he also
played classical music
in the backdrop when he wrote
was a literate man
unlike some Wall street brokers
addicted to making money,
who probably never heard
of Charles Bukowski
or cared about cultivating aesthetics
beyond the supply
and demand for money

You tell me who's addiction
Is More Damning!

Pulling Poems for Inspiration

I wake up early on a Sunday morning
rather distraught and stressed,
another bad dream having come down
from its perch in the Neatherland.

I walk over to my spare bedroom
where the bookcase is cramped
and overcrowded with books of poetry.
I pull Wendell Berry from the shelf
read a poem or two, then turn
my attention to a book of Sharon Olds.

One poem in particular grabs my attention,
about a starving girl in Russia sitting
on the hard ground in the drought
of 1921, stunned, growing thinner
by the day, about to menstruate
with eggs golden as drops of grain,
in the poem- Photograph of a Girl.

It's not the kind of verse I could compose
or have an appetite for writing, but it
gets the cogs turning in my head.

I think back to the text message I
received that night from a friend
in New Hampshire I sent my recent
poetry book and hadn't heard
from until her text told me she
and her hubby, her daughter,
son-in-law and their two-year-old
were on vacation in Nantucket,
and yes, she received my poetry book
but hadn't read it yet.

I got the picture plain and clear,
as a single man with no next of kin,
poetry is not the priority of a friend,
fulfilled with her family and grandchild.
So much for pulling poems off the shelf
for inspiration in my interior world.

The Sound of Waves

I used to listen to the sound of waves breaking
as I sat and ate breakfast at an outdoor café
on Hollywood Beach, Florida.

I would gaze reflectively at the vastness of the Atlantic Ocean,
dreaming of Paris and the Shakespeare and Company Bookstore,
when Sylvia Beach owned it in the 1920's, and a young up and
coming story writer named Ernest Hemingway, an expat from
America, perused the shelves, and Ms. Beach, was eager to let
him borrow books.

Then I'd return to my breakfast of scrambled eggs, home
potatoes, toast, and coffee, which satiated my morning appetite,
before gazing furtively at the ocean, listening to the waves,
watching the orange sun rise on the horizon, before drifting off
again.

Sometimes I'd contemplate whether or not going directly east I
would end up below France near Gibraltar, or farther
south as the map of latitude would lead me.

I never did determine the geography of that, or the means
I didn't have then, to explore the European continent beyond
books and dreams, and besides, the 1920's were some seventy
years removed, warping in the legacy of history books and
backlogs of stories a writer like Hemingway brought back to life
in his memoir-A Moveable Feast.

But those waves breaking on the shore reminded me that time
keeps moving forward, intruding on static motion, and notions
of nostalgia, were impermanent as a passing ship on a journey
through the straits of night, that I could only hold onto for as
long as my imagination permitted.

In the Garden

We make mistakes and that's a given

The perfect poem is a flawed decision

where words dance with despair and hope

in the garden of intent

There is no path to lasting love

Utopia is a state of mind

like Shangri-La behind the lines

Roll the dice in paradise

Something will be

lost and found

in the garden

that you left behind

Change of Seasons

At this point of departure
in the autumn of days
It feels right to retreat by an inlet bay
a waterway heading out to sea
or a running brook in the forest of trees

At this crossroad in the season
there are reasons to be still
not to cling to a spoke
on the Ferris wheel

to reflect on the journey
what was learned on the way

not to harbor resentment
knowing things slip away

in this change of season
to embrace what has changed

Triptych

In her 80's, with a broken hip, and
difficulty getting around, Fleur Byers
persisted with diligence, creating art
with masterful strokes and precision
that inspired me- She passed in 2014,
but her memory lingers on.

--

My late friend Rick Abrams played his
clawhammer banjo to enthusiastic fans,
wrote his prose, and once told me
even if he needed a seeing eye-dog
to get around, he was willing to do a book
tour. Unfortunately, the melanoma took
his life first, but his legacy lives in the
collective memory of his friends and family-
Rick succumbed to his illness at age 47, in 1997.

--

I used to sit outside the Van Dyke restaurant
on Miami Beach with my lawyer friend and
confidant Louis Tertocha, talking about the
music business, trouble in the Middle East,
feasting on food, and the sight of beautiful
women walking past us like eye candy-
Sadly, Louis succumbed to a rare leukemia
at the age of 60 in the Fall of 2013. He is
sorely missed, as are Rick Abrams, and Fleur
Byers.

Bellwether

Winter has arrived early in December
like a flock of sheep over a mountain trek
the leading sheep with a bell on its neck.

The sound is less audible than that of a bell,
more like a muffled engine,
of a snowplow roar.

The white flakes fall steadily
turning the scene
into a tinseled dream.

Those of us lucky enough
to stay home this day
can revel in the view,

but for those outdoors
driving through the haze,
the road is more abrasive.

This is winter's first affair
her cold breath in the air,
a bellwether of the season.

It Is Usually This Time of Year

I begin thinking about Dr. Zhivago, the novel

written by Boris Pasternak.

I surface that scene when the doctor, portrayed

by actor Omar Sharif, is crossing the long cold stretch

of Russian tundra in the severity of winter,

a crippled figure in the cold, as he dreams of Lara Antipova,

portrayed by the young Julie Christie.

Slogging on, icicles formed on his mustache,

his feet frozen in the dense snow, he stumbles,

one step at a time,

wind blowing him about like tumbleweed,

until he finally arrives at Lara's doorstep,

like Lazarus having arisen from the dead,

into her warm embrace,

tracing the agony of love

able to conquer all adversity.

It is this time of year I revisit that script,

and try to persevere through winter's ordeal.

Lester Hirsh Bio

Lester Hirsh has spent nearly five decades performing as a troubadour songster, writing poetry, producing albums of original music, books of verse, a few folk festivals, an editor and publisher of Bone & Flesh literary magazine from 1988-2002, stints as a substitute teacher as well as teaching community education courses on writing, and beginning guitar.

He was a finalist at the Napa Valley Emerging Songwriter Contest, Napa Valley, California in 1997, and nominated for a Spoken Word Grammy in 2005, for selections from his Spoken Word CD, Mosaic ii. Poems of An Ancient Order.

A native of Pennsylvania, originally from the anthracite coal town, Shenandoah, he currently resides in Watsontown. He has also lived in Concord, New Hampshire, as well as in greater Miami Florida, and two years in Tampa. He holds a Bachelor of General Studies Degree, and has been involved with various poetry groups, most notably, The River Poets, in Bloomsburg, Pa.

His poems have appeared in The Asheville Poetry Review, Signal; Coal City; Tabula Rasa; Poetry Ink-The Tenth Anniversary Anthology; Word Fountain; The Weekly Avocet; Bone & Flesh; and The River Poet's Anthologies, Bloomsburg, Pa.

www.ingramcontent.com/pod-product-compliance
Lightning Source LLC
Chambersburg PA
CBHW071516030726
47593CB00003B/1290